Peer Pressure Vs True Friends!

Surviving Primary School Vol. 1

By: Dr. Orly Katz

Illustrations: zofit shalom

About Dr. Orly Katz

Best seller author, Dr. Orly Katz, is an expert for youth empowerment and life skills, who hold a doctorate in Educational Leadership;

She is a sought after guest on TV and radio, and a national speaker and work shop facilitator for parents, educationalists and youth.

Orly is the founder of the "Simply Me" Center for: Leadership, Empowerment and Self Esteem.

Her two book series: Surviving Junior High, and Surviving Primary School, are recommended by the Ministry of Education, and are being taught in many schools as part of the curriculum in life skills lessons.

Orly lives in Haifa, with her Husband and three children.

Please don't hesitate to contact Orly at any time, at: www.SimplyMeModel.com

Table of Contents:

Introduction

The Key to the Environment

A True Story – Crime Doesn't Pay

The Rule for Setting Boundaries

Questionnaire- Do you know how to say "No"?

How do we say "No" and feel good about it?

Energy drains

A True Story - Why We Shouldn't Stay Silent (Or an example of an energy drain called telling tales...)

What is tale telling?

What is reporting?

A True Story True Friends Don't Have Secrets (Or an example about an energy drain called keeping things secret...)

The Rule about Keeping Things Secret

Questionnaire- Do you keep things secret?

A True Story - Painful Fashions! (Or an example of an energy drain called fashions...)

A True Story - The Mean Trick (Or an example of energy drains called rumors...)

Questionnaire - Are you "Stinkers"? (Spreading Tales- or Trash- on the Inter Net about Kids)

The Rule about Rumors

Questionnaire- Do you spread rumors and gossip?

Energy Boosts

A True Story - Couples Dances (Or an example of an energy boost called love...)

The Rule about Love

A True Story - The Outstanding Friend (Or an example about an energy boost called true friendship...)

The Rule for True Friendship

A Story - The Scottish Farmer (Or an example of an energy boost called giving...)

The Rule for Giving

Simply Me- Writing about Myself- Worksheets: The Key to Environment

Questionnaire- Are your friends a bad influence on you?

Summary

Introduction

Dear Readers,

I want to congratulate you on your decision to take action and learn how to survive primary school by joining me in this, the first book of the series!

In each of the four books in the series we discover new keys which together unlock the secret of being 'Simply Me' and together teach you how to believe in yourself and gain self confidence and self esteem.

Anyone in primary school knows just how tough it is:

   -When everyone wants to do something, but you know, deep in your heart, that it's not right for you, but you haven't got the courage to say 'no'......

   -When someone's done something bad to you, but you're scared to report it as you'll be called a 'rat' and then that person carries on doing the same thing to other kids, and won't stop...

   -When people are gossiping about you and spreading rumors to each other and on the internet, and you feel helpless and don't know what to do...

I've got great news for you; it really doesn't have to be like that...

Imagine that you have discovered a secret key "The key to your environment" that will unlock the best way to get through the social maze in primary school:

-How to deal with peer pressure, stand tall and say no!

-How to find who your true friends are, and how to surround yourself with them!

-How to set boundaries, stand up for yourself, and even feel good about it!

-How to deal with gossip and rumors...

-Discover the difference between 'being a rat' and reporting...and exactly when it is important to report something and how to do that

-In brief – how your environment can boost you up or drag you down, and what you can do to shape your environment so that it supports you on your way up.

This book, the first in the series, will help you learn those things that are really important in primary school that no class teacher tells you about. You will discover who your true friends are, how to cope with peer pressure, and most importantly learn how to be "simply me" and survive primary school.

We all have things that we want to say but don't say, we all experience things which make us feel hurt and ashamed and feel that we can't do anything about them, we all remember times that we were afraid of being shouted at, so didn't do what we wanted to do, we all sometimes hide behind a mask pretending to be someone else, someone who isn't really us.

There are times when we get caught up with something and go along with what someone's doing, even when we know it isn't right.

I hope that this book and the other books in the series will help you feel happy with who you are and with what you want to do. You'll come to understand that it needs far more courage to "decide to do what suits me" and be true to yourself rather than being influenced by others and just following on.

The main thing: You'll learn how to be "Simply Me" even if you are sometimes shy, sometimes moody, and sometimes just not quite perfect and come in last...

And you know what? As soon as you truly recognize yourself on the inside, you'll see that something wonderful happens – the people around you start accepting you for exactly who you are too, your friends will understand you, your parents will understand, and most importantly – you'll understand yourself.

Back in the eighties I was in exactly the same situation that you are now...in primary school.

I was scared to stand up for myself, I didn't know who my real friends were, and I had to cope with gossip and with people spreading rumors, and with all those things you are going through now. Until I decided that all this simply had to STOP!

In this book you'll find a lot of true stories about things that happened to me when I was your age...

And if I succeeded in getting through it all, anyone can!

This book will help you do things the best way possible, and gradually you'll discover that something wonderful is happening:

-You'll be surrounded with true friends, who make you feel happy

-You won't be scared of speaking out, stating your opinion and standing up for yourself, even if what you think is different to what other think!

-You'll learn how to free yourself from those things that get you down in primary school (energy drains) and how to surround yourself with all those things in primary school that fill you with energy and boost you up high (energy boosts)!

-Most importantly you'll feel good about who you are, what you do and what you say!

It's really simple!

You'll learn to feel more self confident and to feel good about who you are and about what you do...

Curious?

So how will we do all of this?

As well as true stories, there are helpful tips and fun exercises, quizzes and questionnaires and your own personal journal which you can use to test exactly where you stand in different areas...

I recommend that you don't try to fool anyone when you read the book and fill in the questionnaires and your journal, especially not yourselves.

Answer the questions honestly-there are no wrong or right answers everything is right...

So ...don't you want to start reading?

So, without waiting any more time, let's get started.

Are you ready?
Good luck!
I hope you'll
enjoy it,

orly

The Key to the - Environment

The Key to The Environment helps us to understand how we are influenced by our environment, how our environment can lift us up, or drag us down. We'll learn the difference between the energy drains which are in our environments, which make us feel bad and the uplifting energy boosts which make us feel good.

A True Story – Crime Doesn't Pay

Back in the eighties we didn't have iphones or MP3s but we did have something else, something brand new, something we all were excited about and dreamed of getting.

It was the latest thing and had just come onto the market. The media went wild when it was invented; a new era had begun! You could wear it when you were out walking, riding the bus and go shopping and you could listen to music all the time. Yes, it was none other than the walkman! Today it sounds bizarre, quaint and old fashioned that people got so excited about this invention, but back in those days it was a real revolution. Before anyone in my class actually got a walkman we all knew all about them. They were on the news, there were advertisements for them everywhere, but no-one we knew had actually bought one yet.

Then my lucky day came along.

My father was on the way back from one of his business trips abroad and had been looking for something to buy me from the duty free and had settled on none other than the walkman. I was the first in my class to have my very own walkman!

I was over the moon. I kept the earphones on my head until my ears were burning hot and shone bright red. I had a walkman! I had a walkman!!!

I couldn't wait to turn up at school to surprise everyone.

I knew that all my friends would want to see my new walkman, would want to learn how to use it, would want to try walking, running, hopping and jumping while wearing it. They would all want to listen to it and everyone would talk about it all day long. I knew that I had to bring enough music with me, on what we used to call tape cassettes, so there would be enough music for everyone to listen to. I knew that I was going to be the center of attention. It was all clear…

That's all well and good, but what I didn't know was that I was going to be the center of everyone's attention for quite a different reason to that which I had intended…

It all started going wrong in our second recess. I'd left my walkman in my backpack while I went to buy something from the canteen.

When I got back to the class room I immediately noticed that my backpack was open. I picked it up to close it, but then I saw that all of my things had been moved and my pencil case had been emptied out.

A red light started flashing in my head.

Had someone been going through my things???

Wait a second...what about my walkman??? Had someone been using my walkman????

I checked the side pocket of my backpack where I'd left my walkman...but it was empty. My walkman, my brand new walkman which I had only received the day before-had gone, vanished into thin air! Could someone have taken it?????

I emptied the contents of my bag out onto my desk. My worst fears were coming true. The walkman was gone.

I started to call out to everyone that my walkman had been stolen...that someone had been through my bag and had stolen my brand new walkman during the break.

I can't find the words to describe the heartache, the sadness and the feeling that this wasn't fair that descended on me. You can understand how disappointed I felt (though that's another story) but that was only the beginning.

Every day after that more and more things went missing from our class room- things were being stolen. We were advised not to bring any valuables to school with us, and an investigation was started.

Who could the thief be who was stealing purses, calculators, keys, a walkman (the one and only walkman) and other things too?

As you all know...in the end crime doesn't pay...

One day when we were in gym class B. realized that she had forgotten something in the classroom. She ran back to the room, and found the door closed.

When she opened the door she saw a strange operation was underway. Two girls from the year above us were in our class room. But they weren't just sitting there idly.

One of the girls was standing near the door, supposedly on the lookout-something she failed at miserably, while the other girl was going through all of the bags which had been left in the classroom.

The mystery had been solved...the thieves had been caught, together with all of the stolen goods, or at least most of them!

That isn't the end of the story. When the girls were asked why they had done it the full picture became clear.

The 'lookout' had persuaded the 'pickpocket' to do her dirty work for her, and had got her to go through people's bags, to find their valuables and to steal them. With the money they could buy themselves more and more and more ...designer labels.

The 'lookout' had put a lot of pressure on the 'pickpocket' who hadn't been able to resist and had gradually been caught up in the whole thing. She didn't have the courage to stand up to her friend and she hadn't found the strength to say "no", so she had started stealing for the 'lookout' and ended up paying a very high price indeed!!! Deep down she had known that what she was doing was wrong and as bad for her as it was for the others she had stolen from. She wanted to get caught to put an end to everything she was going through, so she could stop stealing...

The conclusion: Sometimes it's hard to say "no". It makes us feel uncomfortable, we might miss out on something and everyone's doing it, that's what is expected of us.

But there's also a lot to gain from saying "no". We have to be able to set boundaries so we can feel good about ourselves and be completely happy with what we do.

Saying "no" and standing up for your self is a lot braver than doing something just because someone else is making you do it...however nerve-wracking that thing may be.

This is where the 'Key to the Environment' comes into it. The Key to the Environment helps you to understand the influence that our environment has on us, how it can lift us up or drag us down; and how we can set boundaries so that we feel better about ourselves and about those all around us.

The Rule for Setting Boundaries

The boundaries we set enable us to stand up for ourselves, to express our opinion and sometimes simply to say "no" and feel comfortable with it.

Do you know how to say "No"?

Circle your answer for each situation, and add up your score...

	No!	Maybe not	Maybe	Probably	Yes!
You've gone on a trip with the scouts. All of your friends are jumping from a high rocky outcrop into a pool of freezing cold water a long way below. You're scared and don't want to jump. Do you jump?	(1)	2	3	4	5
A good friend wants to come to sleep over. You're very tired and want to go to sleep early. What do you do? Do you say yes and tell them to come anyway?	(1)	2	3	4	5
A kid from your class asks to copy your homework every day. You're fed up of sharing your hard work. What do you do? Do you let them carry on copying?	(1)	2	3	4	5
The popular kids have asked you to come with them to draw some graffiti on the school walls. You don't want to get into trouble and don't	(1)	2	3	4	5

want to go. What do you do? Do you go?					
Your friends have decided to go to the movies, and have chosen a movie that you don't want to see. What do you do? Do you go anyway?	1	2	3	4	5

The Analysis

Add up your scores and find where you fit.

5-11

You certainly stand up for yourself b-i-g time...you say what you think all the time, to everyone. That's good, but you do need to be careful about over doing this sometimes and remembering to be tactful. You sometimes say what you think just because you want to. You need to be careful not to hurt another person's feelings in situations where saying what you think may not be necessary to make a difference.

12-18

You sometimes stand up for yourself and sometimes don't. On the one hand, you know how important it is to be able to stand up for yourself and to say "no" when you need to, and are happy about that. On the other hand occasionally you are still worried about saying "no" and don't always say what you really want to say...My advice: think about what helps you saying "no" in some situations, about how you found the courage to stand up for yourself and what helped you succeed then. You can 'repeat' that courage and do the same thing again. There's no reason for you not to succeed...

19-25

There's no two ways about it...you say yes all of the time. Yes, even when deep down in your heart what you really want to say is "no". You're scared of expressing your opinion if it's different to that held by the majority. You prefer to You prefer to let things go. The main thing is being on every one's good side. You don't want to upset or hurt anyone, you don't want to be different and you don't want to be seen as a trouble maker. I say, go for it. Start small. If you don't want to do something one weekend because you're tired try saying "Not today, I'm exhausted..." and you'll see that nothing happens. Nobody is going to die because of it, and people will treat you with more respect.

So how do we say "No" and feel good about it?

Don't say: "Umm...I'm so sorry...I feel really bad about this...You do understand, don't you?"

Don't say: "Promise not to be cross? Are you sure you're not mad with me? Swear that you're not angry..."

All of that shows that you are not confident with the boundaries you have set.

Just state your opinion with confidence, without apologizing and without arguing!

<u>Energy drains:</u>

Energy drains are all those things in our environment which are bad for us, do us harm or make us get involved with things we don't really want to do. Try to stay clear of energy drains as far as possible.

The next few stories give examples of energy drains in our environment...

A True Story - Why We Shouldn't Stay Silent

(Or an example of an energy drain called telling tales...)

We were about to graduate from elementary school and the PTA decided to organize a special party for our whole year. After long discussions, arguments, suggestions and advice the following was decided: on the last day of school after collecting our certificates we would all have a party at the swimming pool...not any old pool, but the pool at the college leisure centre. The college was fairly near our school, but none of us had thought we would get the chance to swim there until we were older, much older. We all had dreamed of being able to swim at the full Olympic sized pool, with its high diving boards and special equipment for various water sports. The PTA had arranged for us to have the pool to ourselves for the afternoon, with all the games equipment we wanted!

We were excited and started making plans about what equipment we'd use, whether we'd have races and competitions or play water polo or just use the speaker systems for a pool disco. And then of course there were the bathing suits...

When the last day of school arrived we were so excited we almost forgot to worry about our report cards.

The busses arrived to take us right to the doors of the leisure centre, and then after a brief stop in the changing rooms, the fun began.

We started off playing water polo, with the girls playing against the boys. Next we had relay races and then played 'boys against girls' a version of water 'tag' where the girls were supposed to run away (or swim away) from the boys, and the boys were supposed to catch the girls.

What I'm going to tell you next happened to my friend Jennifer, who told me about the incident after it happened, which for some reason sounded all too familiar...

Jennifer told me that Dan had started to swim towards her. She'd tried to swim away as quickly as she could, but he was a much stronger swimmer than she was, so he caught up with her quickly and 'tagged her'. So far so good, but from that moment on things developed in an unexpected way...

Jennifer had been winded when Dan caught up with her, from trying to swim away from him. But Dan didn't just 'tag' Jennifer; he started pushing her down under the water. With what little strength she had left Jennifer tried to swim round Dan under the water and come back up for air, but Dan was there waiting for her, and pushed her head straight back down under the water. Dan wouldn't let Jennifer bring her head up to breathe. She was sure that she was going to be drowned to death!

In the end, after all the air had escaped out of her lungs, Jennifer somehow managed to swim out of Dan's grasp-she had no idea how, and got back up to the surface, pale, breathing heavily, her lungs feeling they were about to explode as she struggled for air, the pain bringing her almost to the point of fainting. But mostly Jennifer's feelings were hurt. Tears prickled the back of her throat, but she didn't want to be thought of as a cry-baby.

The awful fact that Dan had actually tried to drown her, hurt more than the pain of almost drowning. Dan had done something terrible to her for no reason at all.

She didn't understand why he'd done what he did, but she also didn't want the others to know what Dan had done. She didn't want to tell tales, she didn't want to be laughed at, she didn't want to be the girl who spoiled all the fun and in short, she didn't want anything!

Needless to say that Jennifer suffered terribly, albeit in silence, for the rest of the party. She didn't let herself break down and cry. She bit her lip and kept the tears back, suffering from the shame of it all. All she wanted to do was to go home, have a bath and go to bed.

I could see that my friend Jennifer was feeling bad but I didn't know why. I tried to get her to talk to me, and eventually the next day she told me what she'd been through, how she'd almost drowned because of Dan, and then the tears started to flow. But Jennifer remained determined not to tell anyone what had happened. She didn't want to tell tales!

When Jennifer told me about this, I remembered that the very same Dan had done something similar to me the previous year....If only I had reported him to a teacher or any other responsible adult what had happened to Jennifer may have been prevented...

That same Dan had jammed my arm into the central steering wheel of a roundabout during a class get together. He had gripped my arm from above and not let me pull it out. In the end with my last ounce of strength I managed to swing my arm out of the steering wheel. My arm had hung down awkwardly from the shoulder; needless to say I had broken my elbow because of Dan!

I had wanted to shout at him, I had wanted to say that it had been his fault, I wanted to say that he'd hurt me, I wanted to...and I wanted to...but I kept silent as I didn't want to tell tales. If only I hadn't kept silent what happened to Jennifer may have been prevented...

The conclusion:

Jennifer could have spoken to Dan, she could have told him that what he'd done was really dangerous, she had almost drowned, and she could have reported the incident to a teacher or lifeguard, because violence can be stopped.

But Jennifer was frightened that people would think she was being lame, and was especially afraid of being a tell tale, so she kept silent, and allowed the violence to carry on.

You know what, there's an enormous difference between telling tales and reporting!

What is tale telling:

tattle tale.

Telling tales is an energy drain, but reporting isn't.

Telling tales is when someone tells about an incident that doesn't need to be reported, an incident that hasn't caused harm to anyone. (For example when the teacher asks "Who hasn't done their homework?" and someone calls out "Lizzy hasn't...") Telling tales sometimes brings some kind of personal gain, and isn't done to help anyone. It's done to harm or hurt another person or to make them fail.

What is reporting:

An incident is reported when it is something serious that someone responsible must know about: when someone is in any kind of danger, when a law is broken, or when someone is being hurt or is suffering. For example in cases of physical, emotional, verbal or sexual abuse...a responsible adult must be informed, we need to take responsibility and be a true friend by doing the right thing. Reporting can even save lives!

In the case of the incident with me and Dan, I should have reported it and told a teacher. Who knows? Perhaps it was my silence that let him carry on and do what he did to Jennifer..?

A True Story - True Friends Don't Have Secrets

(Or an example about an energy drain called keeping things secret…)

 Naomi had moved to our school when we were in fifth grade. We made friends when the teacher had told her to sit next to me on the very first day of school.

We got on so well…we simply had chemistry. We laughed at the same jokes; we loved sharing bits of gossip together and spent endless hours telling each other fascinating stories…

We spent all of our breaks together, and did all of our assignments together...we were inseparable.

But this inseparable friendship only existed during school hours. Whenever I invited Naomi to come to my house she would make up all kinds of excuses: "I'm busy", "We've got visitors", I need to babysit for my brothers" and all sorts of other excuses. When I suggested that I could come to her house instead she refused point black and it seemed to me that she turned pale at the very idea.

The same kind of thing happened if ever I tried to phone her. In those days we didn't have mobile phones, and whenever I tried to phone her home number it was always unobtainable. When I asked her why that was she told me that they had problems with the line, and it was better if she phoned me.

However the thing that really was the last straw was our class party. In those days we used to have a party for the whole class before Thanksgiving. The party went on late into the night and included a midnight feast. After that we would start telling ghost stories until the middle of the night. Thinking about how late these parties ended gave me an idea. "Let's have a sleep over!" It's a great opportunity and it'll be fun!"

I had never seen Naomi react the way she did to my innocent suggestion. She looked at me furiously, her eyes shining with rage, and she shouted "I'm not coming to the party. I don't want to go".

I knew at that moment that she was lying, I simply knew it.

I knew that she was hiding something from me and I just had to find out what that thing was. I had to finally find out why Naomi would never meet up with me after school, I had to know what was going on and I had to solve the mystery.

I started to put a plan together. That day when my mother arrived to collect me from school I told her about the mystery and asked her to drive slowly following behind the school bus which took Naomi home. In other words I had asked my mother to help me follow Naomi, and an unbelievable thing happened...my mother agreed.

That was how, all at once with no prior warning, we solved the mystery. The school bus pulled up in one of the poorer areas of our town, and Naomi got off the bus.

My mother parked the car and I followed after Naomi keeping a safe distance between us, until I saw the house she went into.

I couldn't really call those slums houses. Many of the windows were boarded up, some of the roofs had tiles missing and the walls seemed ready to collapse at any moment. The 'gardens' were just patches of weeds and there were heaps of garbage piled up around the trash cans.

With my eyes popping out of my head I decided that I had to do something. I walked towards Naomi's house, and went down the path to the front door. I could hear sounds from the other side of the door; a baby crying, and lots of shouting. I knocked on the door and a rather stout woman with her hair wrapped in a rag opened it.

"Hello, I'm Orly, I'm Naomi's friend. Is she at home?"

Guess

"Yes, come on in, please don't mind the mess". She pressed herself to the wall of the narrow corridor so I could squeeze through.

"Naomi, Naomi" she called, "someone's here for you." That's when I saw Naomi as I'd never seen her before. She had one baby balanced on her hip, while a toddler was crawling behind her clinging to her leg. She walked towards me and hissed through her teeth, "What are you doing here?"

"I came to see what you were hiding from me. I came to try to persuade you to come to the party, I came because we are friends and I'm fed up of only being friends during school hours. I want to be your friend after school too. I want you to tell me about your family, I want to visit you at your house."

"So now you've visited it! Do you feel better now?" Tears were glistening in Naomi's eyes and started to flow down her cheeks.

"So now you know all about me! I have five younger brothers and sisters. I'm the oldest who helps my unemployed mum to take care of them. You know exactly what kind of slum we live in, which doesn't even have an indoors toilet. If you need to go…you have to go outside to the shed out the back. You can see for yourself that I don't have my own room with wall to wall carpets and my own stereo like you and your posh school friends have. We don't even have a television, or a telephone. That's why you could never reach the number I gave you…it doesn't exist. Whenever I phoned you it was from the phone box down the street. I don't have a desk to do my homework on. My father works as a porter at the train station and doesn't earn enough to support us all and my mother keeps on having babies. Now you know all of my secrets. Do you feel better now?"

I hugged Naomi with tears streaming down my cheeks. "Do you really think that I like you any less now that I know all that? Do you think that any of it makes any difference to me? I want us to be friends after school too. You can come to sleep at my house whenever you want, and I promise to come and visit you whenever you'll let me come. I only ask one thing...let's not have any more secrets!"

In the end Naomi gradually relaxed, and felt that an enormous weight had been lifted off her shoulders. She came to the party, and even slept over at my house.

As time went by I gradually I realized just how bad it is to keep things bottled up inside, and to keep secrets. Trying to hide things from people and keeping them secret is an enormous burden. The absolute need that no-one should find out 'the secret' drains away all of your energy. For Naomi keeping her secret had been ruining her life. She couldn't join in with anything and spent all her time in fear, worrying about what would happen if anyone discovered her 'terrible secret' of being poor.

Naomi had been so concerned about keeping that secret that she couldn't think about anything else. She couldn't think that perhaps she was hurting her friend- me by keeping that secret- and that she was hurting herself too.

The Rule about Keeping Things Secret

Keeping things secret can drain enormous amounts of our energy. We should try to avoid keeping secrets and have a 'secret free' happy environment!

Do you keep things secret?

Put a circle round your answers for each situation, and add up your score...

The Situation	The Answer				
	Of course not	Probably not	Possibly	Probably	Definitely
Your parents get divorced. Would you try and act as if everything is the same as usual at home, and not tell a single sole?	(1)	2	3	4	5
You're getting towards the end of your schooling but still can't read very well. Would you try to hide this and pretend to everyone that you can read?	(1)	2	3	4	5
You realize you can't see the board in class. Would you try to keep that hidden so you won't have to wear glasses?	(1)	2	3	4	5
You have a handicapped brother who lives in a hostel for children with special needs. Would you keep him a	(1)	2	3	4	5

secret from your friends?					
Your father is made redundant and your family is very badly off. Would you hide this from your friends?	(1)	2	3	4	5

Results

Add up your scores and see where you are in the table

11-15

There's no doubt about it, you're a very open person who tells people things and doesn't hide anything. That's excellent. Just watch out that you don't sometimes share things that aren't relevant to the listeners, who might not need to know absolutely everything. Apart from that, you're doing great, keep it up!

12-18

You're aware of the fact that it's not healthy to keep too many things hidden away. There are some things that you don't share with anyone and others that you are more open about. Try to understand what helped you be open about things in the past and try practicing doing the same with the "big secrets" you hold on to as well. I promise this will make you feel better.

A True Story- Painful Fashions!
(Or an example of an energy drain called fashions…)

I remember our first long hike with our youth club. We were all very proud of our hiking gear. We all had light backpacks, water bottles in case it was hot, waterproofs for if it rained and most importantly hiking boots. We had all been given strict instructions on how to 'break in' our boots; how long to wear them each day for a fortnight before the hike so we wouldn't get blisters. Our parents were going to meet us at the end of the hike for a bonfire and we would get certificates for completing the hike.

We were extremely excited.

I said that we all had our gear...but it turns out that I was wrong. Ruth wasn't wearing hiking boots. She came to the hike wearing smart new Adidas sneakers. Back in those days we didn't all wear 'designer label' clothes and sneakers, and they were still a major fashion statement. She'd just received them from her father. We all gathered round her to admire the sparkling white trainers with the three stripes on each side.

Ruth was ecstatically happy. Our Youth Leader Sheila looked worried. She tried to explain to Ruth that she might have problems wearing the brand new sneakers, but Ruth begged to be allowed to wear them, and Sheila eventually gave in.

The hike got underway. We climbed up and down hills, walked along footpaths through fields and had just crossed a stream jumping over stepping stones when Ruth suddenly sat down, unable to move.

Sheila asked Ruth what had happened. "Nothing" Ruth answered "I'm just having a short rest". We all had to wait for Ruth until she slowly got up stood on her feet and started walking.

Ten minutes later Ruth stopped again. This time she was as pale as a sheet and had tears in her eyes.

"Ruth, we won't make it to the bonfire, stop being such a slow coach" we called out to her.

Ruth didn't say a word. She stretched out her legs, took off her brand new sneakers, or actually peeled them off her feet and showed us what had happened to her.

Ruth's feet were covered in burst blisters with peeled off skin and scabs over dried up blood. Ruth looked at her feet and started to cry.

Sheila turned to her "Ruth, what happened? You insisted on wearing your new sneakers. Why would you want to wear them if they weren't comfortable?

Ruth just carried on crying, and facing down to the ground said:

"They aren't even my sneakers. My father bought them for my younger brother, but I wanted them so I took them for the hike."

Had I heard her right? Ruth had worn her younger brother's sneakers that were too small for her, and hurt her feet just because she wanted to show everyone how cool, up to date and fashionable she was. She had wanted to show off to everyone that she had the newest Adidas sneakers.

Ruth paid a high price for showing off her sneakers!

A True Story - The Mean Trick

(Or an example of energy drains called rumors...)

This story didn't happen when I was your age, as we didn't have internet in those days, but it did happen then just in different ways...

It all started on one perfectly normal afternoon when Claire invited her friend Penny to come to her house. The girls spent the afternoon happily doing things that girls do, laughing, watching television, playing on the computer...until Claire had to go to the bathroom.

What I'm about to tell you actually only took a few moments but the effects were wide reaching and lasted far longer.

The girl's had left Claire's Facebook page open on the computer a while earlier.

As soon as Claire left the room Penny rushed over to the computer and started to write rude comments on the walls of two of Claire's closest friends, Mark and Jessica all in Claire's name. All these comments also showed up of course on the home pages of all of Mark and Jessica's friends.

The first comment Penny wrote was on Mark's wall...Mark was the boy Claire liked then. Penny wrote:

"I've finally realized that you are nothing more than a geeky cry-baby and a nerd"

The next comment was on Claire's close friend Jessica's wall. "Don't you have any fashion sense at all? Your clothes are so ugly they make my eyes hurt. Jessica, do us all a favor and delete the photos you posted last week with that pink shirt you borrowed from your grandma"

Then Penny heard Claire coming back towards the room...

She immediately left the computer, settled herself back on the bed with a book she'd been looking at… with all the skill of a great actress.

The girls didn't look at the computer again during the afternoon.

The next morning when Claire walked into the class room she immediately realized that something was wrong, but she didn't know what it was.

Mark normally greeted her with a stunning grin, but this morning he ignored her, or worse. Claire noticed him whispering something in his friend's ear while he looked at her.

Had Mark suddenly stopped liking her? Was he gossiping about her?

Next, her friend Jessica glowered at her "What's wrong with the way I dress? Since when have you become the editor of Vogue?" Claire looked bewildered. "What are you talking about?" she asked. "You know perfectly well" Jessica replied and continued "If you haven't got anything nice to say, then don't say anything. Now get out of my face..."

Claire didn't know what to do. All day long people gave her dirty looks, ignored her or talked about her behind her back. She didn't understand what was happening and had to fight hard not to burst into tears. All she wanted to do was go home, get into her bed and never get out again.

When she got home from school everything suddenly made sense...

She turned on the computer and opened her Facebook page and saw what her friend Penny (or the girl she had thought had been her friend) had written in her name to her two good friends.

In the end Claire wrote a status so that all of her 783 Facebook friends would know the truth. She explained what had happened, that it had been Penny who had written the comments in her name. Claire wrote that Mark and Jennifer are her two best friends and that she would never do something so awful to them in front of all their friends. She finished her status with a sentence which summed everything up. "It turns out that not everyone who says that they are your friend really is your friend...sometimes they are just jealous..."

The conclusion:

Many people have done this in the past, and many will carry on using the internet anonymously to spread gossip, rumors, insults and anything else to hurt someone using social networks, forums, sites for schools or youth groups...I call them "**Stinkers**" "Spreading Tales on the Inter Net about Kids" and it really does stink!

Think twice before you do something like that...it can always come back at you in one way or another.

Another thing...

The internet is a wonderful way of finding out information, playing games, hearing what's happening, making new friends and keeping in touch with old ones. The internet can be a wonderful energy boost...

But, and it is a very big but, the internet can be an enormous energy drain too when it's used the wrong way, as in this story, or as in so many other stories we hear on the news.

My recommendation: Even though you might think it seems easy to write anonymous comments on the internet, in the end people will find out so don't be "stinkers".

Are you "Stinkers" (Spreading Tales-or Trash- on the Inter Net about Kids)

Situation	Scores:				
	No Way	not likely	maybe	quite likely	Yes!
One of the girls in your class annoyed you to the extreme. Would you spread gossip about her on the internet?	(1)	2	3	4	5
You took an awful photo of someone from behind which makes them look enormous and made you burst out laughing. Would you post it on the net?	(1)	2	3	4	5
You heard a rumour about someone in your year at school, but you're not sure if it's true. You know it will make you more popular if you're the one to post it on the internet. Would you post it?	(1)	2	3	4	5
Your best friend has a crush on the same boy that you are interested in. Would you open a separate anonymous account on the	(1)	2	3	4	5

net to blow her chances?					
You've caught someone at a really embarrassing moment. You're itching to share it with everyone on the net. Would you?	(1)	2	3	4	5

Analysis

Add up your score and see where you fit in.

5-11

Congratulations! Gossip, rumours, anonymous insults just aren't for you.

As far as you are concerned computers, internet, social networks and Facebook are meant for surfing the net, enjoying yourselves and learning new information, not for insults. .Keep it up!

12-18

Sometimes you do feel like getting back at someone on the internet and spreading vicious rumours, but luckily you don't go as far as actually doing it, and that's just as well! You enjoy gossip but are careful as you know there is always the chance that you will be discovered as the anonymous 'stinker'.

19-25

There's nothing to say...you're a real "stinker". You surf the internet on sites like Facebook, and use other forums on the web in a negative way. As soon as you hear any gossip or rumors, or someone has annoyed you, you turn to the web without a moment's hesitation.

A word of advice: take it easy. Things have a way of coming back at you. Also spare a thought for the kids on the receiving end...

Rumors are really unpleasant especially when they are about you yourself!

The Rule about Rumors

Rumors can drain enormous amounts of your energy. Put a hand over your mouth (or keep your hands off the keyboard...), because there is a person behind every rumor and you may fall into your own trap...

Do you spread rumors and gossip?

Circle your answers for each situation, and add up your score...

Situation	Answers				
	Definitely not	Probably not	Maybe	Probably	Definitely
You arrive at school early and head to the cloakroom and see a girl from your class kissing a boy, where they think they can't be seen. Do you tell the girl sitting next to you in class later that day?	1	2	3	4	5
Your best friend makes you promise not to tell anyone their secret. They are in love with your brother / sister. Do you tell them?	1	2	3	4	5
You see a rumour being spread on Facebook about one of your friends. Do you share the	1	2	3	4	5

rumour with the rest of your Facebook friends to be 'in' with hem?					
You get an invitation to join the following group: 'Join this group if you hate ten tonne Hayley'. Do you join?	1	2	3	4	5
During your school field trip you see one of your class mates peeing behind some bushes. Do you tell everyone?	1	2	3	4	5

The results

Add up your scores and see where you fit in the table

5-11

You are a true friend and don't spread gossip, not even behind people's backs. You can be counted on 100%. Everyone would like a friend like you who they can share their secrets with and trust that they will never go any further.

12-18

You enjoy gossiping, but you are careful. From your point of view gossip is harmless fun and you enjoy finding out everything that is going on.
But you also know that people may discover that you have spread rumors about them, so you prefer listening to gossip rather than spreading it further. You might tell some things to your close friends, but not to all and sundry. We just have to hope that the latest gossip won't be...about you!

19-25

It's unbelievable how much you breathe, eat, drink and live for gossip! You know everything, hear everything and tell everything. Sometimes you have to gag yourself. Be careful, you may be your own worst enemy.

Energy Boosts:

Energy boosts are those things in our environment which are good for us, and make us feel happy! Surround yourself with as many energy boosts as possible.

In the following stories we'll see examples of three different types of energy boosts which we can find in our environment (though there are many more).

A True Story- Couples Dances

(Or an example of an energy boost called love…)

I used to love the rainy days in elementary school, even though I'm really a summer person who enjoys sea and sun…

On very wet days we couldn't go outside at recess. The whole class had to stay in the school building. It was boring, we couldn't play 'tag' or soccer or dodge ball or anything else. You are probably wondering why I liked those rainy days so much, you'll soon see…

It's quite simple. We had found a great way to pass the time. That year our school had taken part in a special project teaching us folk dances and we were even going to enter a competition. We had learnt the words to the songs and steps to the dances. At first we had been embarrassed about dancing but soon we started having fun.   Our favorite dance was "Let a boy choose a girl; let a girl choose a boy". A boy stood in the centre of a circle. After we had all danced round him, he had to choose a girl to dance round the circle with. We all knew that the boys always chose the girls that they liked to dance with. Then it was the turn for a girl to choose a boy...

As soon as we saw the day clouding over, the raindrops falling and the puddles beginning to cover the playground, the entire class would gather together near the teachers lounge, ignoring everyone else and start practicing our dances. Sooner or later we would always get around to the dance 'Let a boy choose a girl..."

I had an enormous crush on Steve in those days. I didn't know whether he liked me, I had noticed a few things which made me think that he might, and I hoped from the bottom of my heart that he did, but I couldn't be sure.

Then it was another rainy recess... We started practicing our dances. When we got round to "Let a boy choose a girl", guess what, Steve was the first boy in the middle of the circle. My heart started to race and I could feel it thumping in my chest. I prayed that Steve would choose me. I wanted it to happen so badly. I sung the words as loudly as I could. Steven looked down for a moment, walked towards me and...held out his hand for me to dance with him.

Wow!!! Steve liked me too!!! I was over the moon.

That's all. On that day, the dance "Let a boy choose a girl..." was an enormous energy boost for me...

A True Story- The Outstanding Friend

(Or an example about an energy boost called true friendship...)

Danielle wasn't in my class at school. Our parents were good friends but they lived in a different town. Danielle was a gifted student and was always ready to help others who found things more difficult. She was always there for everyone. She arrived everywhere right on time and was always welcoming when we visited her.

We heard this story from Danielle's mother.

Suddenly, out of the blue, Danielle started being late for school. She would arrive 15 minutes late on good days, and even later on other days.

Her teacher didn't understand what was happening and held Danielle back after school for a discussion, explaining how important it was to arrive on time. Danielle didn't offer any explanations but said she would try to be on time in the future, but she carried on arriving late regardless of the teacher's words.

The teacher tried talking to Danielle again, trying to get to the bottom of why Danielle was suddenly being so late. Again Danielle kept quiet about her reasons and just said she would try.

After a month during which Danielle had missed at least half of the first class each day her teacher called her parents to talk to them about Danielle missing class.

Danielle's mother listened to the teacher and then gave the following explanation:

"Danielle wanted to keep this a secret because she is a good friend, but as I can see that it is beginning to affect her directly I'll tell you what has been going on. Then you'll understand why she is late for school each day".

Danielle's mother started to explain "It is about Michelle".

Gradually as Danielle's mother told the teacher what had happened it all started to make sense, and the teacher began to understand exactly why Danielle was so late each morning.

Michelle was the very spoilt only child of a wealthy family. Her father had been a well known business man who had often appeared in the papers and on the news. He had worked day and night, never taking a holiday or stopping for a break, until one day two years previously he suffered a major heart attack and passed away. Michelle had lost her father.

Fate dealt another cruel blow to Michelle at the start of the year when her mother passed away from cancer. So Michelle was left with all of her money, but without parents.

She went to live with her aunt, her mother's sister, but never adapted to her new life. She stopped functioning. Her aunt didn't know how to cope with her and Michelle simply stopped getting up in the morning to go to school. She was beginning to slide down a slippery slope, letting herself go altogether

That's when Danielle stepped in...

Danielle decided that she was going to help her friend.
Every morning before the first class Danielle would
arrive at Michelle's new home, help her wake up and

coax her to come to school. Eventually, thanks to Danielle, Michelle came back to school and even started arriving on time!

This story is completely true. Daniele was awarded a special prize by the school for being an outstanding friend. She had helped her friend come through a difficult time.

True friendship is a wonderful thing. I hope that in the future my friends will be there for me exactly like Danielle was there for Michelle...

Try to be true friends and surround yourselves with good friends, who make you happy.

The Rule for True Friendship

True friendship is another example of something that can boost our energy. Find out who your true friends are and see how together you can bring out the best in each other!

A Story- The Scottish Farmer

(Or an example of an energy boost called giving...)

Rumor has it that this story is about Hugh Fleming. The story is may be a myth, but it is still a great story...

A long time ago, there was a poor Scottish farmer whose name was Fleming. One day, while trying to earn a living for his family, he heard a cry for help coming from a nearby bog. He dropped his tools and ran to the bog. There, trapped in the mud, was a terrified boy, screaming and struggling to free himself. Farmer Fleming saved the lad from what could have been a slow and terrifying death.

The next day, a grand carriage drew up outside the Scotsman's small farm house. An elegantly dressed, wealthy landowner stepped out and introduced himself as the father of the boy Farmer Fleming had saved. "I want to repay you," said the wealthy man. "You saved my son's life."

"No, I can't accept payment for what I did," the Scottish farmer replied, refusing the offer. At that moment, the farmer's own son came out of the door of the tiny family home.

"Is that your son?" the grateful landowner asked.
"Yes," the farmer replied proudly.
The man said, "I'll make you a deal. Let me pay for his education. If he is anything like his father, he'll grow to a man you can be proud of."

In time, Farmer Fleming's son graduated from St. Mary's Hospital Medical School in London, and went on to become known throughout the world as Sir Alexander Fleming, the discoverer of Penicillin.

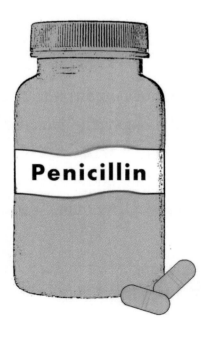

Years afterward, the wealthy man's son was stricken with pneumonia.

What saved him? Penicillin...

There's a saying "What goes around comes around". If you do something good, something good will happen to you.

I wish you much happiness through giving.

The Rule for Giving

Giving generously is another example of a way that we can boost our energy. If we make giving part of our environment we actually get far more back in return...

Writing about Myself-
Worksheets:
The Key to Environment

1. When you say "Yes" what exactly do you mean?

Have you ever said "Yes" although you really wanted to say "No"?

Describe the incident.

What was the result and how did you feel?

_____

_____

_____

2. When you say "No" what exactly do you mean?

Have you ever said "No" although you really wanted to say "Yes"?

Describe the incident.

What was the result and how did you feel?

_____

_____

_____

3. Peer Pressure- past and present:

Think of a recent occasion when you experienced peer pressure:

Describe the incident.

How did you cope with it?

_____

_____

_____

4. Advantages and Disadvantages of Facebook and Social Networks

What are the Advantages of Facebook and Social Networks?

1._____

_____

_____

2._____

_____

_____

3._____

_____

_____

4._____

_____

_____

What are the Disadvantages of Facebook and Social Networks?

1._____
_____
_____

2._____
_____
_____

3._____
_____
_____

4._____
_____
_____

5. My Rulebook

Write down ways to stay safe when using Facebook and Social Networks:

1._____

2._____

3._____

4._____

5._____

6._____

6. Bullying, physical and verbal abuse, exclusion and isolation:

Have you ever been bullied in any way?

1. What happened?

2. How did you feel when it happened?

3. What did you do when it happened?

7. Bullying, physical and verbal abuse, exclusion and isolation- a personal experience:

Share a personal incident which you experienced where you were either actively involved in some form of bullying. Or you were amongst the onlookers who saw someone being bullied:

1. What happened?

2. What did you do when it happened?

3. What would you do differently now?

8. The Difference between Reporting and Telling Tales:

Have you ever wanted to report something to a teacher, but didn't because you were scared you would be accused of telling tales?

1. What exactly happened?

_____

_____

_____

2. What was the end result?

_____

_____

_____

9. True Friendship:

What does true friendship mean to you?

1. How do you choose your friends? What is important to you?

_____

_____

_____

2. What characteristics should someone have to be your friend?

_____

_____

_____

3. Have you got true friends?

_____

_____

_____

Are your friends a bad influence on you?

Draw a circle round the answer which best suits each situation for you and then add up your score...

	Definitely not	Probably not	Perhaps	Probably	Definitely
Your friend got hold of a copy of the questions that will appear on the next day's test. Can you resist the temptation and avoid looking at the questions?	1	2	3	4	5
Your younger brother has stolen some chewing gum. He asked you not to tell your parents as he will get into trouble. Would you tell on him?	1	2	3	4	5
You found a wallet with a large sum of money in it. No one saw you find it. Would you hand the wallet over to the police without taking any of the money?	1	2	3	4	5

	1	2	3	4	5
Your friend wants to put glue on the teacher's seat to make a fool of her. Would you tell him that there's no way that you'd go along with the prank?	1	2	3	4	5
Your friend tells you that he is going out with two girls at the same time, and that neither one knows about the other. Would you tell him to be ashamed of himself?					

The Analysis

5-11:
You're not on the right path. You don't mind stealing and cheating and your friends influence you in bad ways. It's time to change your habits and fast before you get into serious trouble.

12-18:
You actually want to be 'bad' but fortunately haven't got the courage to do anything too bad. Don't let your friends influence you and get you into trouble. It could get seriously out of control.

19-25:

You're good through and through. You're not influenced by your friends. You have a strong character and believe in justice. Honesty pays in the end.

We can't finish without a short summary:

Dear friends,

We've come to the end of the first part of our journey towards 'discovering myself'. I wanted to thank you for coming along for the ride, so together we could make some important discoveries on that important question 'how can we survive primary school?'

This book is the first in the series of books which together can help you learn, and practice until they become second nature, those things that are really important to know in primary school. It explains those things that you've always wondered about, and wanted to know, but class teachers just don't explain.

This book has introduced you to 'the key to your environment' which has let you into the following secrets:

-How to deal with peer pressure, stand tall and say no!

-How to find true friends who really make you feel happy! How to surround yourself with more and more friends.

-How to set boundaries, stand up for yourself and cope with peer pressure, and even to feel good about being able to say 'no'!

-How to free yourself from all those things in Junior High that get you down (energy drains) and how to surround yourself with things that give you the energy to reach for the sky (energy boosts)!

Most importantly you discovered who you really are, standing tall, living above the influence, being true to yourself and learning to feel good about who you are and what you want and what you do!

Together we learnt to understand the influence our environment has on us, and how our environment can either lift us up or drag us down. We saw what we should do in order to shape our own environments so that it supports us as we move on up.

By using this key which is so, so simple you can feel happy, contented, satisfied, charming, beautiful, rich, wonderful, clever, cool, popular, loved, amazing, admired, hypnotizing, awesome, astounding, brilliant, cute, charismatic, hot, wicked, cool dudes, positive, friendly, sought after, sexy and everything else....

Seriously now:

Using this Key will help you to simply be you...who you really are and to feel good about yourselves and with what you want and with the things you do.

All I have left to say is that I hope you enjoyed reading this as much as I enjoyed writing it.

Now...it's time to get busy...all you've got left to do is to start practicing everything...so .get started!

Wishing you all things good,

orly

Thank you for purchasing this book!

It is very important to me to get your feedback and hear what you think!

Please write a review on Amazon and let me know your thoughts.

Other Books by Dr. Orly Katz:

peer pressure vs. true friends!
Surviving Primary School Vol. 1

Be Positive! Think Positive! Feel Positive!
Surviving Primary School Vol. 2

Body Language, Intuition & Leadership!
Surviving Primary School Vol. 3

Passions, Strengths and Self Esteem-
The Extensive Guide!
Surviving Primary School Vol. 4

Other Books by Dr.Orly Katz:

peer pressure vs.true friends!
Surviving Junior High Vol. 1

Be Positive! Think Positive! Feel Positive!
Surviving Junior High Vol. 2

Body Language, Intution & Leadership!
Surviving Junior High Vol. 3

Passions, Strengths and Self Esteem-
The Extensive Guide!
Surviving Junior High Vol. 4

Made in the USA
Middletown, DE
19 December 2018